Searching For Treasure:

The Coloring Book

By
Marty Elwell

Illustrated by
Steve Rose

THE FAMILY LEARNING SERIES

NOBLE PUBLISHING ASSOCIATES

GRESHAM — OREGON

Noble Publishing Associates

Noble Publishing Associates, the publishing arm of Christian Life Workshops, is an association of Christian authors dedicated to serving God and assisting one another in the production, promotion, and distribution of audio, video, and print publications. For instructions on how you may participate in our association, or for information about our complete line of materials write to: NPA, P.O. Box 2250, Gresham, Oregon 97030 or call (503) 667-3942.

ISBN: 0-923463-85-2

Printed in the United States of America.

DEFINING WISDOM

But everyone who hears these words of mine and does not put them into practice is like a foolish man who built his house on sand. The rain came, the streams rose, and the winds blew and beat against that house, and it fell with a great crash.
- Matthew 7:26,27

BECOMING WISE

At Gibeon the Lord appeared to Solomon during the night in a dream, and God said,
"Ask for whatever you want me to give you."
- I Kings 3:5

RECOGNIZING THE WISE MAN

But Daniel resolved not to defile himself with the royal food and wine,
and he asked the chief official for permission not to defile himself this way.
- Daniel 1:8

THE FOOLISH MAN

But Rehoboam rejected the advice the elders gave him and consulted the young men who had grown up with him and were serving him.

- 2 Chronicles 10:8

CHOOSING YOUR FRIENDS

When Delilah saw that he had told her everything, she sent word to the rulers of the Philistines, "Come back once more; he has told me everything." So the rulers of the Philistines returned with the silver in their hands. Having put him to sleep on her lap, she called a man to shave off the seven braids of his hair, and so began to subdue him. And his strength left him. - Judges 16:18,19

BEING A FRIEND

In the morning Jonathan went out to the field for his meeting with David. He had a small boy with him, and he said to the boy, "Run and find the arrows I shoot."
- 1 Samuel 20:35,36a

HONORING YOUR PARENTS

So he said to them, "Why do you do such things? I hear from all the people about these wicked deeds of yours. No, my sons; it is not a good report that I hear spreading among the Lord's people. If a man sins against another man, God may mediate for him; but if a man sins against the Lord, who will intercede for him?" His sons, however, did not listen to their father's rebuke, for it was the Lord's will to put them to death. — 1 Samuel 2:23-25

CONTROLLING YOUR ANGER

Now Cain said to his brother Abel, "Let's go out to the field." And while they were in the field, Cain attacked his brother Abel and killed him.

Genesis 4:8

GIVING UP YOUR PRIDE

Suddenly the fingers of a human hand appeared and wrote on the plaster of the wall, near the lampstand in the royal palace. The king watched the hand as it wrote. His face turned pale and he was so frightened that his knees knocked together and his legs gave way.

- Daniel 5:5,6

OVERCOMING TEMPTATION

Again, the devil took him to a very high mountain and showed him all the kingdoms of the world and their splendor. "All this I will give you," he said, "if you will bow down and worship me." Jesus said to him, "Away from me, Satan! For it is written: 'Worship the Lord your God, and serve him only.'"   - Matthew 4:8-10

ARGUING AND COMPLAINING

The Lord said to Moses and Aaron: "How long will this wicked community grumble against me? I have heard the complaints of these grumbling Israelites. So tell them, 'As surely as I live, declares the Lord, I will do to you the very things I heard you say: In this desert your bodies will fall - every one of you twenty years old or more who was counted in the census and who has grumbled against me.'"
Numbers 14:26-29

GOSSIPPING

When the Jews in Thessalonica learned that Paul was preaching the word of God at Berea, they went there too, agitating the crowds and stirring them up.

Acts 17:13

LYING

Peter asked her, "Tell me, is this the price you and Ananias got for the land?" "Yes," she said, "that is the price." Peter said to her, "How could you agree to test the Spirit of the Lord? Look! The feet of the men who buried your husband are at the door, and they will carry you out also."   *- Acts 5:8,9*

BEING WICKED

Ahab said to Elijah, "So you have found me, my enemy!" "I have found you," he answered, "because you have sold yourself to do evil in the eyes of the Lord. 'I am going to bring disaster on you. I will consume your descendants and cut off from Ahab every last male in Israel - slave or free.'"
— I Kings 21:20,21

CHEATING AND STEALING

Achan replied, "It is true! I have sinned against the Lord, the God of Israel. This is what I have done: When I saw in the plunder a beautiful robe from Babylonia, two hundred shekels of silver and a wedge of gold weighing fifty shekels, I coveted them and took them. They are hidden in the ground inside my tent, with the silver underneath."- Joshua 7:20,21

PLOTTING EVIL

So Haman got the robe and the horse. He robed Mordecai, and led him on horseback through the city streets, proclaiming before him, "This is what is done for the man the king delights to honor!"

- Esther 6:11

SEEKING REVENGE

"See, my father, look at this piece of your robe in my hand! I cut off the corner of your robe but did not kill you. Now understand and recognize that I am not guilty of wrongdoing or rebellion. I have not wronged you, but you are hunting me down to take my life. May the Lord judge between you and me. And may the Lord avenge the wrongs you have done to me, but my hand will not touch you."
— 1 Samuel 24:11,12

GOODNESS AND MERCY

Her mother-in-law asked her, "Where did you glean today? Where did you work? Blessed be the man who took notice of you!" Then Ruth told her mother-in-law about the one at whose place she had been working "The name of the man I worked with today is Boaz," she said.   *- Ruth 2:19*

GIVING AND BEING GENEROUS

She went away and did as Elijah had told her. So there was food every day for Elijah and for the woman and her family. For the jar of flour was not used up and the jug of oil did not run dry, in keeping with the word of the Lord spoken by Elijah. — 1 Kings 17:15,16

WORKING HARD

From that day on, half of my men did the work, while the other half were equipped with spears, shields, bows and armor. The officers posted themselves behind all the people of Judah who were building the wall. Those who carried materials did their work with one hand and held a weapon in the other, and each of the builders wore his sword at his side as he worked. But the man who sounded the trumpet stayed with me. - Nehemiah 4:16-18